Other books by
Stewart S. Warren
www.heartlink.com

Powers
&
Patterns

Powers
&
Patterns

poems from the

Tarocchi de Mantegna

Stewart S. Warren

Powers & Patterns:
poems from the Tarocchi de Mantgena
Copyright ©2014 Stewart S. Warren

ISBN: 978-1-940769-10-3
Publisher: Mercury HeartLink
Printed in the United States of America

Mercury HeartLink
www.heartlink.com

SOCIAL STATIONS OF HUMANITY

Wretch
Servant
Artisan
Merchant
Gentleman
Knight
Duke
King
Emperor
High Priest

NINE MUSES AND APOLLO

Calliope
Urania
Terpsichore
Erato
Polymnia
Thalia
Melpomene
Enterpe
Clio
Apollo

LIBERAL ARTS

Grammar
Logic
Rhetoric
Geometry
Arithmetic
Music
Poetry
Philosophy
Astrology
Theology

CARDINAL VIRTUES

Intelligence
Time
Cosmos
Temperance
Prudence
Strength
Justice
Charity
Hope
Faith

HEAVENLY SPHERES

Moon
Mercury
Venus
Sun
Mars
Jupiter
Saturn
Eighth Sphere
Prime Mover
First Cause

ACKNOWLEDGMENTS

There are so many mentors in this age and in ages past, so many willing to lend a hand. I am connected, held in place, and encouraged to reach higher by each and every one. For this I am grateful.

The deck presented here, whether created by Andreas Mantegna or Ludovico Lazzarelli, has its roots in the Renaissance with connections to the Classical Era and the mystery schools of antiquity. Because studying this tarocchi from several perspectives will aid understanding, I have included three introductions by competent Tarot historians and enthusiasts. At first glance we notice an overlap in their descriptions of the architecture of the Tarocchi de Mantegna. But this is not redundancy, rather the unique perspective of each contributor as they offer interwoven views that reinforce the intelligent design of this powerful teaching tool.

Each review, or mini essay—from England, Italy and France—provides the reader with context and pertinent cues that one might receive from a tour guide as they enter an ancient temple of higher learning and spiritual celebration.

It's my pleasure to present, not only examples of the work of others, but to encourage the reader to investigate these writers and explore more of their expertise in the areas of history, sacred symbolism, and mystical experience.

My thanks go to. . .

OSVALDO MENEGAZZI from Il Meneghello publishing house and Tarot shop in Milano, Italy graciously provided permission to use card images from the *Tarocchi de Mantegna . [color enhancements by the author]*
Visit artist, printer and Tarotist Osvaldo Menegazzi and his family at Il Meneghello shop on 12 Via Fara in Milano.
—www.arnellart.com/osvaldo.

SIMON WINTLE from the Isle of Anglesey, UK, along with Adam Wintle, is curator of the *World of Playing Cards* and *The English Playing Card Society* websites, dedicated to the history and visual art of playing cards.
—The World of Playing Cards—www.wopc.co.uk

MORENA POLTRONIERI, historian, writer and Tarotist, is co-founder and curator of the Tarot Museum in Northern Italy, and has co-authored many books on a variety of esoteric topics, as well as art guides to European cities.
—www.museodei.com

PATRICK COG, Editions SIVILIXI, is restorer and publisher of antique Tarot decks from the 17th Century. He is also the author of "*The Mysteries of the tarot of Viéville, decoding an esoteric tarot of the XVII century*" in two volumes exploring both the Major and Minor Arcana of that historically important and hauntingly beautiful pack.
—Editions SIVILIXI, www.editions-sivilixi.com

SARAH OSBORNE, editor from Bristol, UK has provided splendid Italian to English translations for this book and other Mercury HeartLink publications.
—sarahosborne765@gmail.com

for those
who desire to receive
for the sake of imparting

A Humanist World View
by Simon Wintle

The so-called "Tarocchi di Mantegna" is a set of 50 copper-engraved emblematical images (c.1465) which were probably a social pastime, or an instructional or educational series designed to awaken spiritual enquiry. It is not clear whether they were produced by Andrea Mantegna (1431-1503), however, the subjects of the set are mentioned by Giorgio Vasari who writes in his Lives of the Artists that Mantegna created copper prints of "trionfi", another name for the tarot Trumps.

There are no suits and the images are numbered consecutively from 1 to 50, divided into the following groups: Society; Apollo and the Nine Muses; the Arts and the Sciences; the Seven Virtues and Sun, Time and the World; the Planets and the Spheres. Thus we have a system of divine activities and functions reflecting an ideological structure and a social hierarchy within it.

Different versions and copies of the engravings by various artists reveal some differences of detail, suggesting that the ideas were open to interpretation. Stewart Warren's poems included in this volume further open the mind to unseen realms.

Of the known examples none were made into a pack of playing cards, but were printed onto thin paper as black and white outlines. However, woodcut copies of these engraved images occur in later educational or didactic books.

Undoubtedly this deck represents a humanist world view of the day; the outward design and hierarchical structure, beginning with the fool and leading via craftsmen to the aristocracy, the king and the pope, through the muses, virtues and planets to the Cosmic Principles, reflects an androcratic, neo-platonic ideology.

Maybe the tarot trumps were merely an alternative or condensed version of these images, which most educated people would recognise, added to a pack of cards for the purpose of making a new card game. On the other hand, perhaps the mystery is in the silence behind the thoughts.

— Simon Wintle

Revealing the Mysteries
by Morena Poltronieri

Through these Tarot Cards history has left its indelible mark; one which is not always decipherable or understood. Many have attempted to define these works of art, starting from the Italian Courts of the Renaissance, from which these fascinating emblems appeared, overlooking the tradition that has safeguarded them for centuries in the collective mind.

In order to understand the significance of the arcana, simply remembering them is not enough. One's imagination can often be deceptive, and knowledge limiting, in so much that one needs to draw upon all these elements together. Employing all of the senses and breaking with tradition, is to understand the mystery that touches and animates existence.

Fragments of the same symbols, the Tarot Cards trace history; they describe the myth and teach how to see merely beyond looking. They don't uncover: they reveal. Their shadowy veil is not one that obscures, but protects. And, thanks to this body of work by Stewart Warren, we can close our eyes and trust ourselves to listen. We can hear the ancient canticles, those which hide a secret code linked to man's existence. And from the canto (derived from the word 'incanto', to mean 'enchanting') the poem becomes accessible not only from understanding the Tarot, but from hearing them also.

One enters into a resonance which informs the connection with the Universe, not only when the sublime is reflected in the Earthly, but also when parts of a continuous evolution exchange. The image becomes word and, as we know, the word creates. In this way are we able to enter into the Hermeticism of the Tarots by a door through which Stewart Warren guides us, opening within the poem's core, a reflective quality.

In Greek *poiêtês*, or rather 'poet', is someone who creates, who generates new worlds, leaving behind those which exist. The *Tarot of Mantegna* is one of these worlds— created in 1467 in the Ferrara area—they recount the *The Human Condition*; in other words how human beings, during their time on Earth, encounter it. It represents the relationship between the divine spark and the incarnation with its rules, and eventually the systems through which we need to elevate ourselves.

We encounter the Muses, the realms of Arts and Science and, most importantly, Apollo, God of the Sun, of Medicine, of Prophecies and of Music. More cantos and enchantment. The poetry becomes one with the image, colouring it, transforming it, making it translucent; breathing life into it. Without effort, we absorb it, so that its essence focuses on one single moment; that which we are living. A suspension between different universes, that Mr. Warren unites with his poetry and which resonates inside of us.

We do not, however, believe that this suspension distances us from reality. On the contrary, it is described to us and the *Liberal Arts* present in this pack of Tarot Cards represent a treasure trove. Contained inside is theoretical knowledge that essentially the human being is free, and therefore accountable. Only in this way can we reach the *Spirits* and the *Virtues,* then the *Planets* and the *Stars* of the Universe. And, finally, the *Eighth Sphere*, the *Prime Mover* and the *First Cause*, that is to say, God.

In other words the 'home-coming', that is where we leave behind the day. As with these Tarot Cards life also loosens itself through circularity; where the beginning and the end meet, continuing without an end. These emblems and this poetry remind us that we are not just a drop in the ocean but we are rather of the ocean. Everything is one. And even when we are no longer here on this Earth, the images and the poems will continue to describe history... ours also: from that of the highest level to that of the lowest.

— Morena Poltronieri

AN INITIATIC VOYAGE

BY PATRICK COG

Stewart S. Warren, who has already published poetic collections on three magnificent ancient tarot decks, now presents us with his latest work, "Powers & Patterns" the fruit of his inspiration on an exceptional tarot, the Tarocchi del Mantegna.

The Tarocchi del Mantegna is a very unusual tarot, compared to the too few ancient tarots which have survived the ravages of time. In this 15th century deck, we find neither the usual structure of 22 arcane majors nor the four series of minors. Those readers familiar with the tarot of Marseille may at least recognise some familiar cards such as the Emperor, the Pope, Temperance, Strength, Justice and the Moon and the sun. It is to be hoped that readers are not put off by this aspect of the Mantegna.

Therefore, rather than being discouraged by this aspect, it is hoped that the curious scholar will marvel at this surprising succession of fifty cards, which start with MISERO, a poor man in rags leaning sadly on his stick, and ending with PRIMA CAUSA, an image of the ancient cosmogony where the earth is the centre of the universe. Faced with such a succession of cards, surprise gives way to delight. Right from the start, we discover a social hierarchy in the first ten cards. The miserable beggar— the lowest condition—is followed by the servant, the tradesman, the merchant, the gentleman, the knight, the doge (or first magistrate), the king, the emperor and the pope at the height of the human hierarchy. The ascending and descending aspect of this hierarchical succession is a fascinating discovery: the pope has certainly the highest function which is the most difficult to obtain, contrary to the beggar whom fate has thrown into the dirt, but who represents the immense majority of humanity, whereas there is only one pope! These first ten cards show us not only a representation of the caste system, and allow us to contemplate an elevation by merit on the terrestrial social ladder; but also the opposite mechanism, the idea of karma: regression due to misbehaviour.

Here we find one of the profound mysteries of this tarot, because apart from the first arcane, MISERO, is it not an idyllic representation, as if evil didn't exist? It is necessary to imagine a kind of reversed Mantegna tarot, where a virtue expresses its opposite. Thus the tradesman suggests its antithesis, bad workmanship; the king, the tyrant; the pope, the antipope; and so on for all the cards, except, without a doubt, for the last two, unalterable.

However "Le Monde" (the world) is not just a mundane social ascension or its opposite. This tarot is not limited to the first ten cards, and from the cards XI to XIX, we find a series of nine muses. These muses appear to represent that which inspires man's soul, what makes him greater and what fleetingly reveals his own divinity. Then the twentieth card reveals Apollo, mediator between the gods and man, who brings the Olive branch to the world. It is Apollo who introduces us to the Sciences with the next 10 cards, and we notice that the ancient scientific hierarchy is respected because Astrology and Theology are respectively the twenty ninth and the thirtieth card, the last two of this series of ten.

This progression continues with the cards XXXI to XXXX where we can see the ten emotional and intellectual qualities which allows man—*homo sapiens*—to live, control and progress in the social dimension of human life. It would be more accurate to say nine emotional and intellectual qualities because this series of ten cards finishes with FEDE, Faith, which is an intrinsically spiritual quality.

Thus this card XXXX introduces the last series of ten cards, a cosmic and super-human series, with the seven planets of the antique world, or its occult equivalence, the seven planetary regents; then OCTAVA SPERA, the superior heaven, "the World of the Divine Spirit, without form"; then PRIMO MOBILE or *Fohat*, "The living Force created by WILL"; and finally PRIMA CAUSA, the eternal cause, or "He who cannot be spoken about".

Can we imagine a more intriguing journey than that offered to us by the Tarrochi del Mantegna, an initiatic voyage where through fifty stages we experience the expanse of divine creation? By sublimating matter and unifying the earth and the heavens, where "what is up high is like what is down below and what is down below is like what is up high", this exceptional tarot invites us on a transcending journey.

With *Powers and Patterns*, Stewart S. Warren, an admirer of beautiful tarots, invites us to discover the Tarocchi del Mantegna, guiding us poetically through the fifty steps of this cosmic temple. Through rhythms and rhyme, we become immersed in a universe of unspoken messages, represented by the images of the tarot. We linger on the questions that it raises, and on the infinite mysteries that the card, seemingly a closed and finite universe, conceals.

—Patrick Cog

Powers
&
Patterns

WRETCH

Half naked and ashamed,
I rest a dull head
on my hand, my hand
on earthbound staff.

The dogs and I do what we do,
the wall in disrepair.

I ponder my predicament and place.
Vaguely it occurs to me
I don't know
what I don't know.

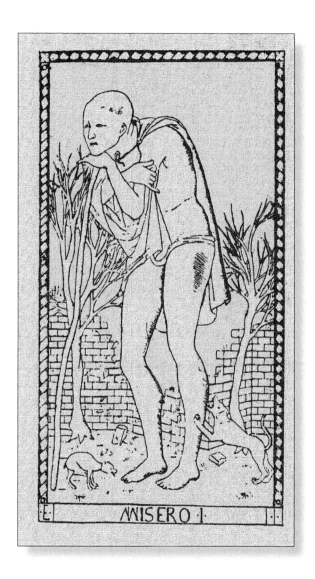

MISERO I

STATIONS OF HUMANITY

SERVANT

Uncertain in myself
I approach, bring gifts at times
I feel unworthy to receive.

Though the contents
of this cup seem sealed,
I begin to wonder
what this vessel has
to do with me?

E · FAMEIO II · Z

ARTISAN

I set to it, prompted now
more by desire than necessity,
to become an instrument
in the making.

I fashion a fire in my stove
and direct it so.
Beauty is a power
that wants to multiply—
she stands behind everything I do.

ARTIXAN · III ·

MERCHANT

Numbers don't lie
but liars can figure
as I move the world
from town to town.

Where others are concerned
I have a certain edge,
but real justice is clean
and far above me.
I have a choice in how I deal.

MERCHADANTE IIII

E · 4

Gentleman

With the dogs now in tow
and my falcon
in service to my wants,
I find good manners
is smart going.

I mimic the gestures
of an emperor.
Time now for cultivation.

Knight

We distinguish ourselves
with weapons, conquer
in the name of this or that,
play with symbols of power,
ride with intoxication.

I myself have converted thousands
by the sword.

E · CHAVALIER · VI · 6

STATIONS OF HUMANITY

DUKE

The fertile colors of my robe
are my face upon the earth,
evergreen, ever giving,
ever done from the womb.

Behind the façade
of my monk's hood
the eternal mystery of ages.

Look deeper here.

·DOXF. VII·

E   ✝

STATIONS OF HUMANITY

KING

My feet are unshod
but rarely touch the ground,
my rule an approximation.

In my court it seems
that deeds are done
according to weight,
measure and favor.

If you question fairness
you question temporal rule.

·RE·VIII·   E   ·8·

EMPEROR

Authority flows here
as a robe over the stairs
of our successive stages.
The sky is our reach.

Gods and goddesses dine with us.
We converse on matters
of church and state,
but wonder
who stirs above us.

IMPERATOR · VIIII ·

E·   ·2

High Priest

10 and **1** are one and the same.
You've reached me
through the others, though
now you know to begin with me.
These words are heresy.

The book opens, turns
its own pages. These keys
have always belonged to you.

·PAPA·X·

E · 10

STATIONS OF HUMANITY

CALLIOPE

This is how we'll communicate—
not a thing to mean another thing—
but through the music
of words, initial sounds
cascading in consort.

Dreams fly through the windows
of your own making,
the poetry of a shell
uncurls within you.

Share wisdom with others.

·CALIOPE·XI·

MUSES

Urania

You are the confluence
of the constellations.
Record your nights
that you may keep your days;
live freely tethered to their pull.

They are lights
on a stairway to unseen realms.

· VRANIA XII ·

D   IZ

Muses

TERPSICHORE

How glorious to move as a body,
as river song, as snake,
as storm, as stone.

The body life is dance—
all the way up, all the way down.
Deny nothing that is truly
inspired and enthused.

This vehicle is cosmic.

TERPSICORE · XIII ·

MUSES

ERATO

Rising up through the rush of us,
I am the sweat of the desert mixed
with firelight, skin, clinking bells.
Lose yourself here, my darling,
for you are nothing alone.

Crawl to me growling
that I may thrust you
into night's fire.

ERATO · XIIII · D 14

MUSES

POLYMNIA

Each life so unique,
so heroic. How brief
these flowers on the hill,
how unrecognizable
after last year's thaw.

Sing of them, each one,
how their leaves reached
for the light, the proud way
their petals fell.

We are story on this road.

· POLIMNIA XV ·

D   IS

MUSES

Thalia

When dressing for the festival
choose a face that fits the feeling.
Whom do you wish to be?

Skip as lightly as you will,
though you may find
the chilling face of another
deep in the well,
and yet... another.

·TALIA·XVI·

D·   ·IG·

MUSES

Melpomene

There's no shame
in shying from pain,
but when it's your turn
in the barrel,
show your shadow inside out.

Let the rest of us know
we're not alone.
The beauty of the mountain
is in her tear-carved canyon.

MELPOMENE · XVII 17

MUSES

Enterpe

Each tree, street corner,
bowl and loaf,
every double-ended moment,
gives forth a song.

I listen with body and soul
to the opera of us,
and also the part I play.
All given together,
not a note out of place.

·EVTERPE·XVIII·

D | 18

MUSES

CLIO

This is our river today,
the course of it just as it is—
this great moving moment
is our state of affairs.
Find yourself here.

The golden past is gone;
the undetermined future fickle.
I will crown you
at the end of this day,
and not on another.

·D· ·CLIO·XVIIII· ·19·

MUSES

APOLLO

Mastery begins in surrender.
Even the goddesses and gods
must reckon with the wind.

East and west determine my center;
I give the eagles reign and claim dominion.
In the midst of my shining—
the dark sun of sadness.

I hold all things as one.

·APOLLO·XX·

D·   ZO

MUSES

Grammar

Cliffs and waves rise from the ocean,
stand in relation to one another.
So too each grove of trees
makes sentences of meaning
as they lean and crouch
and run for the sun.

Comprising a word
is equally sublime. But ah!,
the emanation and quality
of a single letter.
G

·GRAMMATICA· XXI

Liberal Arts

LOGIC

False memories built
on pride and fear
hinder my purpose.
I deconstruct to reconstruct.

If I desire to know
the harmony of things
I am therefore the word,
blooming as a rose,
fulfilling a greater purpose.
Is this not so?

C   LOICA XXII   Z

LIBERAL ARTS

Rhetoric

With letters and logic
I present to you the cosmos of me.
And on occasion I've been known
to believe what I think.

All this is posture and practice
for an age when with words
I will design new worlds—
a compound operation
of incantation, magic and reason.

· RHETORICA XXIII ·

LIBERAL ARTS

Geometry

Soon you'll see them everywhere,
plane, solid and exalted—
sound, shape, relationship.

Be a Merkabbah
cutting through time
to bring the princess home.
Use love and light
in your constructions.

GEOMETRIA XXIIII

LIBERAL ARTS

ARITHMETIC

Some say, Release A to arrive at B,
others count their way there,
put their roads in a row.

You may like to count
by touching fingers,
but it's ratio, ratio, ratio.
Never lose sight
that one plus one is three.

·C· ·ARITMETRICHA·XXV· ZS

LIBERAL ARTS

Music

Follow the watercourse
high into the hill
where choir upon choir
make themselves known.

It's true, a song was here
before we came, so our joy
is joining with others.
Take pleasure in music
and the false will fall away.

·MVSICHA XXVI

POETRY

Before prose was poetry.
Before reason, the music of the mind.

There is nothing so wise
as the curve of a swan,
no cure so complete
as the tides that sway within us.
Court her with awe
and uncertainty.

Mystery is the door.

·C· ·POESIA XXVII· Z7

LIBERAL ARTS

Philosophy

I come as lover, as friend,
as servant to thee.
I live by your light
in the simplest of ways—
on the coast with nets,
at the table with children,
on the street buckling and bold.

Investigation is the simple right of all.
Only later
do we surround ourselves
with books of books.

·PHILOSOFIA·XXVIII·

LIBERAL ARTS

ASTROLOGY

And now I understand
that to study the travels of geese
north to south, or winds west to east,
is to suspect the same forces
that move daylight and stars.

I am caught inevitably
in these invisible currents,
purposeful swirling
of humanity and worlds.

·ASTROLOGIA·XXXVIIII· C 39

LIBERAL ARTS

Theology

I study god and goddess as I please.
Is there any other inquiry?

New recipes and rituals appear
as children make up
story after story.
You discover some truth
in every myth—and here
I afford you the gift of silence.

THEOLOGIA · XXX ·

C· 30

LIBERAL ARTS

Intelligence

Diamond radiance, giver
of light, life and love,
I wear your clothes
and a piece of your mind.

Self reflective now, a keen fire
has been lit, chain reaction
of internal combustion.

The knower has awakened.

B. · ILIACO · XXXI · 31

CARDINAL VIRTUES

TIME

Bracelet of pearls, sequence
of worlds, rings of fire going round.
I take time to my bed, this friend;
we woo one another.

I feel my way through her,
swallowing and swallowed.
Within this suspension
all is death and rapture,
a moment to repent, to return.

·B· CHRONICO XXXII 37

CARDINAL VIRTUES

Cosmos

Sometimes the all is small,
within the palm of your hand,
pulse of blood, galactic center
passing through.

As thought must have mind,
so must I have you.
There is no location—
except here—that can be found.

·COSMICO·XXXIII· B 33

CARDINAL VIRTUES

TEMPERANCE

Rock, paper, scissors;
it's one eclipse after another.

We shape each other,
hold the human tribe in line.
I withdraw my inappropriate gesture
or I lose my hand.

I am formed,
and formed again, still higher.
Balance is operation and law.

·B· ·TEMPERANCIA·XXIIII· B+

CARDINAL VIRTUES

PRUDENCE

To know myself
in the machinery of us
I examine what I was before.
There is movement
in all our clawing and scratching,
something vital, innocent.

To move forward I must forgive—
it is then I am delivered,
made ready again.

PRVDENCIA·XXXV

CARDINAL VIRTUES

STRENGTH

My vitality is a burning rose,
a raging sex, a snow plow at 70.
Her teeth are practiced.

If I run, she springs from a ledge.
My strength, then,
is the intelligence of love.

FORTEZA·XXXVI

·B· 36

CARDINAL VIRTUES

Justice

This one looks me in the eye.
I tried wielding her sword
but it was heavy
and I was sloppy.
There is blood on this trail.

Sooner or later,
we learn to kneel.
It is for this
that time is our friend.

·IVSTICIA· XXXVII· B 37

CARDINAL VIRTUES

CHARITY

Are we not nature?
Are we not one with all others?
There is this single breath
passing between us.
Feed the birds.

Feed the birds.

·CHARITA·XXXVIII· B 38

CARDINAL VIRTUES

HOPE

The solar genius has not dimmed.
You have transcended yourself
untold times. By a thousand names
she leads you on,
by infinite means
she unfolds this song.

Always, and all ways, onward.
Catch this wave.

SPERANZA · XXXVIIII ·

B 39

CARDINAL VIRTUES

FAITH

Freedom of will is but consent.
He gives us his heart
and we begin to understand.

This is the invisible bread,
inexhaustible good,
ours by right of birth.
Lean into it, pilgrim.

FEDE·XXXX·

B 4○

CARDINAL VIRTUES

MOON

You were my first teacher,
first love.
I can only speak of our secrets
in number and song.

You are woman and man
and howling haunt.
All that I feel
sways in your passing.

LVNA·XXXXI·

41

COSMIC SPHERE

MERCURY

Closest stone to the sun,
you're a quick study.
What you know is delivered
on language with wings;
the silver distance,
the in between.

My personal guide,
I dedicate this book to you.

MERCVRIO XXXXII · | ·42

COSMIC SPHERE

Venus

Before the switch,
you were the tough guy,
regent of radiance, warrior and such.

We could use a love like that—
someone to cut a swath
through all this selfishness,
establish beauty above all else.

·VENVS XXXXIII· A 43

Cosmic Sphere

SUN

Oh, the reach of your embrace,
the pulse of your nurturing gaze.

Our family seems to float here
all alone. But as all parents know,
there are winds and weather
beyond the next rift.

As protector
you ready yourself
at the helm.

SOL · XXXXIIII

A·   44

COSMIC SPHERE

MARS

Now's the time for your ferocity.
Turn, not against us
for we have slaughtered our own,
but with us
through the approaching threshold,
another run at kingdom's gate.

Champion us, captain,
into our inevitable paradise.

COSMIC SPHERE

JUPITER

If it weren't for your wandering ways
you'd be a star, fixed
with your celestial friends,
casting expansive spells.

As it is, you carry our goodness
across the black dust.
You are the whirling pride
of humanity, our personal
beacon into the night.

· IVPITER · X X X X VI · | 4C

Cosmic Sphere

SATURN

For one without age
your image looks stern and faded.
But you are forever young,
quick, ubiquitous.

I'm dying to know
where your children have gone.
Harvest, indeed!

·A· ·SATVRNO·XXXXVII· ·47·

Cosmic Sphere

EIGHTH SPHERE

There are seasons,
and there are seasons.

I feel them in my bones,
in the lighted wings of my mind,
on the soft skin of my soul.

I feel these braided ropes twisting
through the heavens of us.

·A· OCTAVA SPERA · XXXXVIII ·48·

COSMIC SPHERE

PRIME MOVER

Behind all suns, another one.
Who moves here?
All music, art, the invention of zero,
spirals pecked on rock,
every vowel lifted aloft... all
in praise of you.

Tell me, who is it that moves?

CoSMIC SPHERE

First Cause

It cannot be found out there,
nor conquered in here.
All ideas fail, not even this
silent whisper can tell.

I would say—You are this.
I would say it forever,
but I don't yet fully know
what this means.

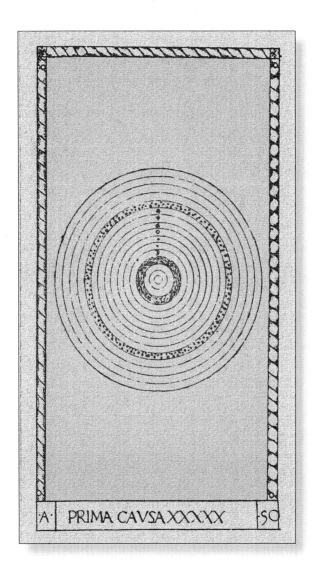

PRIMA CAVSA XXXXX

COSMIC SPHERE

Made in United States
North Haven, CT
16 November 2022

26798066R00073